AOTEAROA NEW ZEALAND

Faces of the land

AOTEAROA   NEW ZEALAND

Faces of the land

PHOTOGRAPHS BY
HOLGER LEUE

TEXT BY
WITI IHIMAERA

REED

First published in 1995 by Reed Books, a division of Reed
Publishing (NZ) Ltd, 39 Rawene Road, Birkenhead,
Auckland. Associated companies, branches and
representatives throughout the world.

Text © Witi Ihimaera and Reed Publishing 1995
Photographs © Reed Publishing 1995

ISBN 0 7900 0407 0 modern
ISBN 0 7900 0430 5 traditional

Project coordinator: Ian Watt
Editor: Susan Brierley
Cover and text design: Chris Lipscombe
Text set in Adobe Garamond 3 and Frutiger.
Colour separations, printing and binding by
Everbest Printing Co, Hong Kong.

Half-title page: Chris Kohere, East Cape.
Title page: Road and rail bridge near Kumara, West Coast.
Imprint page: Fiordland crested penguins, Monro Beach, West Coast.
Contents page: A young East Coast farmer takes smoko, a break from his work.

For my dear friends.

— H.L.

For Jessica and Olivia Ihimaera-Smiler.

— W.I.

Contents

The land at the end of the sky

NEW ZEALAND IS THE LAND at the end of the sky. We are where the sky slopes down to the crisp crystal dome of Antarctica, at the southernmost extremity of the world. You can't go much further south than us. We are the last whistle stop before you hit the ice.

There are days when the beauty of New Zealand can take your breath away, days when you can believe that God must surely live here. Fire and ice conjoin here, earth and water, sea and sky, all the elements in opposition to create a unique world. In the north the coastline is a golden sickle stretching onto forever; in the south it becomes a place of fiords which one of our early writers impishly described as looking a little like a piece of cheese whose edges had been bitten around by mice.

Within this compass of land, sea and sky are the New Zealanders. The Maori say we were fished up by a demi-god, Maui. Our Maori ancestors settled here and made New Zealand — or Aotearoa — the southernmost tip of the Polynesian triangle; Hawaii is the northern point of the triangle and Easter Island near the coast of Chile is the

'KIA ORA!' East Coaster Raewyn James, the back of her car filled with farm supplies, stops to wave on her way back from shopping in town.

eastern point. For the Pakeha we were never quite the Great Southern Land that everybody hoped for — the huge southern continent which was supposed to balance the northern hemisphere's European and American continents. But we were a place where people could bring their ideals and dreams from the failed dark spaces of the north. A Dutch explorer found us, the French considered settling us, but it was the British who stayed on.

One and a half centuries after Maori and Pakeha signed the Treaty of Waitangi in 1840, we have become a country of independent and strong-willed people. We have also become a Pacific Rim people with a strong attachment to our front yard, the South Pacific Ocean. We are proud of our status as New Zealanders and we are great defenders of our sea.

There is no doubt that we have been great plunderers of the northern cultures, retreating with our booty to our island fortress far to the south. Our cities of Auckland, Wellington, Christchurch and Dunedin — and our international tourist towns like Rotorua and Queenstown — offer as much in terms of technology, business acumen and cosmopolitan sass as anywhere else in the world. The melting pots which are our cities throw us all into the same space and make a mockery of boundaries. This is the country where you can reach the Prime Minister by picking up the telephone. The housewife with children is just as likely to be found in the fabulous coffee houses of Ponsonby as the television celebrities of 'Shortland Street'. Although class and race distinctions exist, New Zealand society is too much on the move, too much in flux, for these to have become entrenched.

You can see great art, great theatre, great movies in New Zealand — and you can read great books. New Zealand's own creative men and women include people like Katherine Mansfield, Colin McCahon, Dame Kiri Te Kanawa, Janet Frame, Sir Howard Morrison and Patricia Grace. You can watch great sport, pretend you are Sir Edmund Hillary and go climbing peaks in the Southern Alps, surf the wild waves of the East Coast or take a jet-boat ride down the Shotover River. You can also experience great scenery and, particularly, the culture of the Maori and Polynesia, in the largest Polynesian country in the world.

We are also a very youthful country. This youthfulness, and the exuberance that comes with it, has made us a mix of 'aw shucks' innocence combined with experience and a very strong sense of where we want to go and who we want to be. It has contributed to the good old 'let's have a go' spirit. We are young enough to take risks. We are not so old that we always tread carefully. It is this ingenuous side of the New Zealander which helps to push us forward when others might hold back and which balances the sober face we sometimes present to the world.

This is our country.

This is us.

Tenei matou.

A FISHERMAN and his dog take a break at the Hokianga Harbour, Opononi, Northland.

Ra whanau i a koe! Happy birthday to you!

WHATEVER THE CULTURE, the passages in life are there to be celebrated — and nobody is too old to have a birthday party. In Maori culture, for instance, you are still a youngster at fifty, or sixty in the case of Moengaroa Kerei, whose birthday cake combines whimsy with aroha (love).

The Maori, who comprise ten percent of New Zealand's population, are one of the most characteristic faces of the land. Sometimes warm, always passionate about the land, fisheries and cultural issues, Maori are building a society which will take them into the 21st century.

Here, at Moengaroa's birthday, however, they take a break from life. Get the whanau, the family, around. Put down a hangi. Have a good feed of crays. Sing a little. Dance a lot. And laugh.

The hangi or earth oven is the traditional way of cooking food. Heated stones are placed in a deep pit and doused with water to make steam. Baskets of food are placed in the oven, covered, and the oven is closed to seal in the steam. The secret is in the timing. If you uncover the hangi too soon the food is not cooked properly. If you take it out too late, it is overcooked. But if you time it just right, the food is succulent and superb.

I refuse to grow old any way but reluctantly and bold as brass.

— Bub Bridger, poet

'GIVE US A HAND, EH?' Moengaroa Kerei's family prepare the birthday feast, including the hangi (earth oven) and a bucket of fresh crays, at Te Kaha, East Cape.

Now THAT the kai is cooked, and everybody is in the dining room, let's get into it!

A FATHER HOLDS his daughter at Moengaroa Kerei's birthday celebration.

People of the land

So who are the New Zealanders? Perhaps it shows in our faces. Not only are we Maori but also Asian, European, Polynesian or African and, most often, a blending of many heritages.

We are also, of course, more than what our origins show us to be. For instance, although half of New Zealand's three and a half million people live north of the Bombay Hills (between Auckland and Hamilton) we are also a people of the land and sea.

The quintessential 'good keen man' is still around, but you are more likely to find him riding a moped than a horse, stalking deer by helicopter and talking into a cellular phone as he goes about his work. The happy go lucky Maori has turned into an astute businessman or woman with a calculator in one pocket and taking a degree in business on the side.

All this has made the faces of New Zealanders a wonderful blend of spirited and shy, dark and light, innocent and experienced, youthful and old. Don't be mistaken, however: New Zealanders have an edge. We are an articulate, astute people with a deep sense of politics and of rightness. The state of the nation is a constant subject of conversation as we attempt to solve internal issues and our relationship with the rest of the world.

Here, then, are the people of the land.

The Maori call us tangata whenua.

MAN OF THE EARTH and sea. Hilla King, Kaikoura.

Mana Kilaroa Malcolm, Kaikoura, and Melissa McKenna and her dog Holly, near Hastings.

SERGEANT RAY SMITH, Auckland, and Maninderjit Singh Sandhu, Queenstown.

Paradise ... blue water, blue sky and a bold yacht

OF ALL NEW ZEALAND cities, Auckland is often referred to as being the most 'American'. It is also New Zealand's largest city, and home to an amazing array of New Zealanders.

Perhaps Auckland's greatest wonders are its harbour, beaches and the fabulous islands of the Hauraki Gulf. No-where is New Zealand's pride in its maritime history and its competitive spirit more evident than in Auckland. At least a million boaties go out onto the harbour every summer, to sail craft of all shapes, sizes and descriptions.

The yacht, however, is king, sailing against a background of Auckland's sky-piercing waterfront.

New Zealanders… spend their lives wanting to set out across the wide oceans that surround them in order to find the rest of the world.

— John Mulgan, novelist

YACHTS JOSTLE and sway in Westhaven Marina, crowned in the distance by Auckland Harbour Bridge.

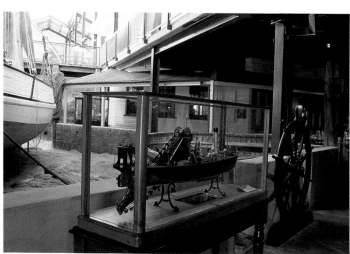

PORT OF CALL. Four views of Auckland's harbourfront, a place of bustling ferries, the Harbourside Restaurant and the Maritime Museum at Hobson Wharf.

A GREAT WAY to get around! Tandem cyclists pedal past the Ferry Building, Auckland.

THE FUN DOES NOT stop at night. Queen Street is busy, buskers enthral the crowd at Hobson Wharf, and at the nearby Oriental Market a Chinese New Year celebration.

A KALEIDOSCOPE of lights and entertainment. The City of Sails lights up across the water at evening, the highrise buildings like sails in the darkness.

MORE CITY SIGHTS — drummers invoke a hypnotic beat on Princes Wharf, Auckland.

The Topp Twins are an institution in the bars and coffee houses of Auckland.

Down in Christchurch, the Wizard enchants the crowd in Cathedral Square with his own magical brand of spells and invocations.

FURTHER SOUTH, at Bluff, Fred and Myrtle Flutey show off their paua shell house.

IT'S A TRY! Dreaming of wearing the All Black jersey, Junior All Blacks play rugby at Little River, Banks Peninsula.

Rugby league supporters proudly back the local team at Carlaw Park, Auckland.

'KA MATE, KA MATE! Ka ora, ka ora!' Young Maori boys, under strict tutelage, practise the men's haka at Apanui School, Te Kaha, East Cape.

The most magic word to me was still Imagination, a glittering noble word, never failing to create its own inner light.

— Janet Frame, novelist

THE GIRLS enjoy playing titi torea, a Maori stick game.

Hold fast to your Maoritanga

NEW ZEALAND IS THE ONLY COUNTRY in the world where you will find authentic Maori culture. Thus, it is a taonga, or treasure, which gives New Zealand its distinctive personality. Everywhere, Maori people maintain their culture, but particularly on their marae (home place) where genealogy, discussion, music, traditional dance, carving and other arts are practised.

One of the great centres of Maori culture is the Maori Arts and Crafts Institute in Rotorua, established in the 1920s to provide a school of learning for Maori craftsmen and women. Apprentice carvers can be viewed practising their time-honoured craft.

The Institute adjoins Te Whakarewarewa Thermal Reserve where, in an area only 1 km long and 500 metres wide, more than 500 hot springs bubble and spurt, and geysers shoot hot steam toward the sky.

A MAORI GUIDE welcomes a visitor by pressing noses. A whalebone hand weapon, feather cloak and wooden carving show the sophisticated arts of the Maori.

HAERE MAI, HAERE MAI. Within Te Whakarewarewa Thermal Reserve is a Maori Village complete with palisades, carved meeting house, foodstores, canoes and sleeping quarters. Locals still use the thermal pools for cooking, washing and bathing.

TE TAKINGA MARAE, near Rotorua. At the apex of the meeting house a carved Maori warrior holds a taiaha (fighting staff) in the posture of challenge. Right, a detail from the intricate carvings which adorn Te Takinga meeting house.

'Gidday there!' Farmer Owen Maru sells produce to travellers from his trailer near Pipiroa, Thames Valley.

JOSEPHINE TREANOR, from Pipiriki, on the Whanganui River, shows off her paraoa rewana bread. Baked in a heavy iron pot, 'Maori bread' is leavened with potato yeast.

At Katikati, in the Bay of Plenty, the side of a fish and chip shop has been painted with the portraits of local people.

WAY DOWN SOUTH in Riversdale, Southland, butchers Graham Goombes and Graham Young take a break from serving customers prime Southland beef.

I suppose the reason people talk about the good old days is that they're so pleased to have got through them.

— Fred Dagg, alias John Clarke, humorist

NO, IT'S NOT a lawnmower. Try, instead, an antique farm machine that Mum can drive, on display at the Vintage Machinery Festival, Fairlie.

NOTHING LIKE a refreshing draught. At the end of a hot day at Fairlie, a farmer cools down with a good cold beer.

Kiwi ingenuity on the Coromandel

AT DRIVING CREEK, on the Coromandel, potter Barry Brickell has indulged his lifetime fascination for small-gauge railways to create a thrilling miniature railway ride which winds up through brilliant green bush to a magnificent view across the Coromandel valley.

Barry Brickell is one of New Zealand's best-known and respected potters. He has made at Driving Creek not only a miniature railway, but also an artists' community. In a cluster of workshops, potters young and old come to work the Coromandel clay.

The Coromandel Peninsula is one of New Zealand's most prized areas, with breathtaking beaches and ever-changing vistas of lush green forest, red pohutukawa, golden sands and rock formations, and sparkling bays.

CREATOR BARRY BRICKELL at his work as a potter, and pottery and railway in artistic juxtaposition.

Driving Creek's railway repair yard and siding show the enormous amount of work required to make sure the trains keep on schedule.

ALL ABOARD the Driving Creek express!

To keep tiny flies out of a safe, keep a small spider in one corner. Put a few grains of sugar in every other day, and he will keep your safe free of tiny flies in return for an undisturbed home.

— Aunt Daisy, pioneer commercial broadcaster

AH, THE GOOD OLD DAYS before supermarket shopping. Tins and packets of produce on display at the Shantytown Store near Greymouth, West Coast.

THESE WOMEN are only too happy to serve you and have a bit of a chat at the Op Shop, Coromandel.

A PIG SEEMS to have strayed into a cattle herd near Te Kao, Northland.

THE SAME GOES for this caravan, in the middle of cows grazing near Waima, Northland.

SOME RURAL WHIMSY — a cow mailbox at Whangateau, on the Kowhai Coast, north of Auckland, and a sign warning that a native pukeko may be crossing the road at Le Bons Bay, Banks Peninsula.

ANYBODY AT HOME? A goat shelters in an oil drum at Inglewood, Taranaki.

KIWI COWBOY Mark Williams and his dog Zack herd cows from a three-wheel-drive near Fox Glacier.

THREE SHEARERS, one rousie and a dog, Lynvale Farm, near Te Anau.

Grow up, oh young and tender plant

WHO CAN EVER FORGET their first day at school? The classroom. The other children. The new teacher. Things don't change much at all, especially in rural schools throughout New Zealand.

The school bus stops at farm gates along the way to pick everybody up. By the time it reaches schools such as Ruatoki School, in the Bay of Plenty, it is full. There's just time to play for a while before the school bell summons you to assembly. And after assembly it's on with the business of acquiring learning and those skills which help us with our careers — and with getting on with the rest of our lives.

Children are our greatest treasure. Whether they are Maori or Pakeha we want them to grow up strong and to grasp in their hands all the skills they will need to achieve their destiny.

THE SCHOOL BUS arrives at Ruatoki School, Bay of Plenty. Children have a lesson outside their classroom; inside is a display of their art.

'GROW UP, oh young and tender plant. Grasp in one hand the treasures of your ancestors, in the other the tools of the Pakeha. Look to God who is the giver of all things. Make a topknot worthy to place like a crown on your head.'

— translation,
Sir Apirana Ngata

A STUDY IN black and white on green, as bowlers at Gore, Southland, watch a drive to the other end of the bowling green.

THREE IN A ROW, as young Highland dancers perform at a Pipe Band festival, Napier.

So what's up with spaceship earth today? Noted adventurer and columnist Wendy Brown catches up on the news at Cafe Cézanne, Ponsonby, Auckland.

RICHARD HORDER is more down to earth as he talks about life as skipper of the scow *Nellie*,
Abel Tasman National Park.

'IS THIS SEASON better than the last?' Farmers and breeders look over the stock and consider making a bid at a livestock auction at Coroglen, Coromandel.

A FARMER CONSIDERS his options at the livestock auction.

A MILKMAN makes deliveries in Lyttelton, where home delivery is still a tradition.

CATTLE ON THE MOVE, this time at Kohukohu, Northland.

Shaped by the sea

THE PACIFIC OCEAN or Te Moana nui a Kiwa — the Great Ocean of Kiwa — is the largest ocean in the world, and New Zealand is at its southern gateway. Everything that is here has had to come across the sea.

When you fly across the Pacific from Honolulu, below is a vast marine continent scattered with islands. By day, the sight of that ever-spreading ocean is awesome. Early settlers conquered that distance, first the Maori in sea-going canoes from Tahiti, and then the Pakeha in sailing ships from the northern hemisphere. The fears of sailing, of life and death on the high seas, resonate in the waves which beat the New Zealand coastline.

There is no doubt that New Zealand — and New Zealanders — have been shaped by the isolation imposed by the sea. Distance has been conquered but the sea continues to roll out of our past into the present and forward into the future — a reminder of Nature's uncontrolled magnificence, sometimes warm, sometimes wild, sometimes 'gone weirdly pale jade' or startling blue.

No place in New Zealand is further than half a day's drive from the sea. It is not to be wondered at, therefore, that New Zealanders love and respect the sea so much. It sings in our soul.

It is our bounty as well as our pleasure.

We are islanders.

THE SEA SWEEPS IN at Castlepoint, in the Wairarapa.

ALONE ON THE BEACH at Okarito, Westland, as the moon rises over the Southern Alps.

WAITING FOR the big wave. Surfers Shayne Stirling and Hamish Johnstone, Oreti Beach, Southland.

VISITING HONEYMOONERS look out over historic Akaroa Harbour, Banks Peninsula.

THIS BEATS WORK — bathers soak in the warm pools that they have scooped out at Hot Water Beach, Coromandel Peninsula.

REAL OR ILLUSION? A mural of Aotearoa, painted on a blank concrete wall in Wakefield Quay, Nelson.

Sunday at the beach

A BRITISH HUMORIST once said that he came to New Zealand but it was closed. Well, the reason for this was that New Zealanders have always valued — and still value — their weekends. And in summer, wouldn't you rather be at the beach?

When New Zealanders think of playing or having fun, they think of either beaches or mountains, both of which we have in abundance.

Family beaches abound around the coastline, normally not so far from the city that the children will get tired of travelling there and back. Many beaches are patrolled by surf lifesavers like the two above, seen at the Otago Surf League Championships, St Clair, Dunedin. Surfers, sunseekers and those who want to get away from the crowd go to more remote beaches, where often you can be alone with nobody else in sight.

Whatever you desire in a beach can be found. So pack up a picnic, throw a few cans of drink in the walking pack, put in the towels and some walking gear, and don't forget the sunscreen. And have fun.

LIFE IS A BEACH. Surfies start out to the beach. Meantime a volleyball game is already underway, and a surf lifesaver from St Kilda watches over the beach.

GO, MAN, GO! A surf lifesaver makes for his surf ski at the Surf League Championships, St Clair, Dunedin.

I am never confident I can win a race until I've reached the stage in it where I absolutely know I can't lose.

— Sandy Barwick, marathon runner

THE BOUNTY OF the sea. Oyster farmers bring their catch to shore near Ohope Beach, Bay of Plenty.

WAY DOWN AT the bottom of the South Island, things are quieter at Half Moon Bay, Stewart Island.

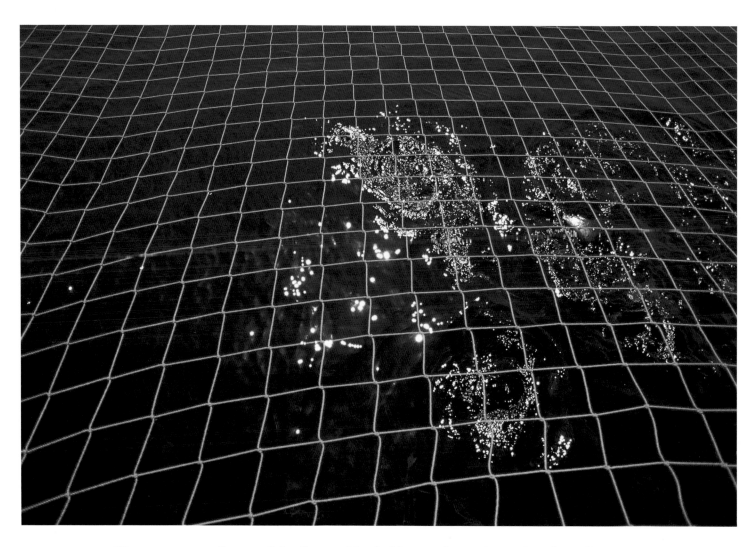

NOT FAR AWAY, at Paterson Inlet, Stewart Island, things are happening at the salmon farm.

IT'S BEEN ROUGH out there. A fishing boat makes its way through Paterson Inlet, Stewart Island.

Fishing net, Moeraki.

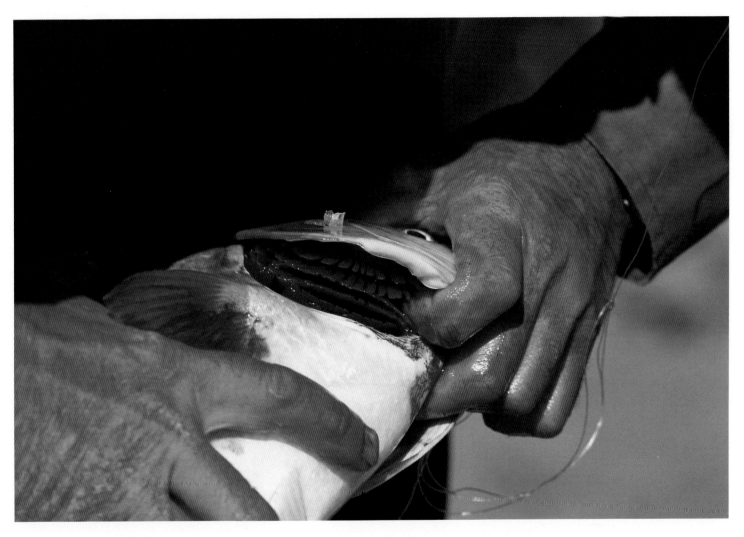

KAHAWAI CATCH — a fisherman removes his hook from a kahawai, caught at the Moeraki
Peninsula.

Aboard the *Milford Wanderer*

ONE OF THE best ways to see New Zealand is from the sea. When you're down in Fiordland there is no other way, because much of the spectacular beauty of the Sounds is inaccessible by road. So what better than to take a voyage on the *Milford Wanderer* (above), and recapture the romance and spirit of a bygone seafaring age?

One of the most haunting of the southern fiords is Doubtful Sound, named Doubtfull Harbour by Captain Cook in 1770 because he was unsure that the HMS *Endeavour* would be able to enter and exit the somewhat narrow entrance.

Dusky Sound, New Zealand's largest fiord, is entrancing. Remote and unspoilt, it is worth the journey just to see the teeming bird life and dolphins. Here, light and colour appear as they must have at the very beginning of the world.

SKIPPER JAMES KING-TURNER welcomes you aboard the *Milford Wanderer*.

ON THE BOWSPRIT, a sailor keeps a watchful eye. A petrel soars across the sombre water of Dusky Sound and below, sharks are hauled aboard.

A PLAYFUL DOLPHIN leaps before the *Milford Wanderer*, scouting ahead across the mist-enshrouded sea.

EARLY MORNING mist,
Doubtful Sound.

Always to islanders danger is what comes over the sea.

— Allen Curnow, poet

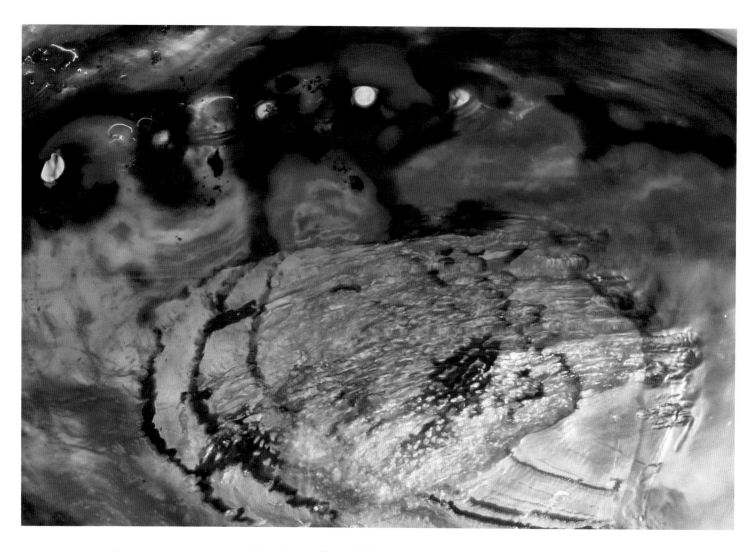

IRIDESCENT BEAUTY — the colours of the rainbow are caught by the sea and held in a paua shell.

ON A BEACH near Opotiki, two Maori seek the succulent pipi.

WHERE SUMMER LIVES —
Awaroa Inlet, Abel Tasman
National Park — a beautiful
coastline, broken granite
country, strands of golden
sand and offshore islands
floating in an impossibly
azure sea.

Pohutukawa trees, Opoutere, Coromandel; when the trees flower well they signal the coming of a long hot summer.

CATHEDRAL COVE, near Hahei, Coromandel Peninsula, is noted for its pink sand, pohutukawa trees and, as embellishment, a giant Moreton Bay fig.

POHUTUKAWA FLOWERS blossom at Punakaiki, West Coast.

THE FASCINATING Pancake Rocks at Punakaiki.

Okarito, place of magic

ONCE, MINERS RUSHED to Okarito to look for gold. From 1868 to 1907 the township was quite something, with pubs, dance halls, casinos, banks and stores all doing great business.

Today, Okarito — and Okarito Lagoon — is more of a place of spells and enchantments woven by land, sea and sky. World renowned novelist Keri Hulme (pictured here with Bill Minehan) has described Okarito with all the sorcery of her language in her prize-winning novel *the bone people.*

At Waitangiroto Stream, near Okarito Lagoon, is the only breeding ground of the stately white heron, or kotuku. The kotuku has always been regarded with awe by the Maori because of its rarity, loveliness and grace in flight.

Whitebait also bring Coasters down to places like Okarito. When the whitebait season opens, men and women trail nets in an almost religious frame of mind. It is one of the events by which Time is marked on the West Coast.

Art to me is — catching on paper or in some construct a thought, a face, an idea, a dream. I don't draw true landscapes; I try to delineate inscapes for others to see.

— Keri Hulme, author

ABEL TASMAN monument, Okarito

WHITEBAIT, FISH and stones — the patterns of Nature, at Okarito.

A LONE CANOEIST and a white heron share the beauty of Okarito Lagoon.

A LOAF OF BREAD, a jug of beer, a whitebait net and a good season — that's all you need in Okarito.

FROM OKARITO with love. The eternal whitebaiter casts his net; the Southern Alps are seen from Okarito Trig Point; cyclists stop awhile to revel in Okarito's natural beauty. Later, what cosier way to enjoy friends and good company than around a bonfire under a silver moon?

FOR CENTURIES the Maori used flax for clothing, baskets, nets, mats and medicine. This plantation is at Harihari, West Coast.

THE FAMED MOERAKI BOULDERS, each weighing several tonnes, are said to be the petrified food baskets of a legendary canoe which was wrecked on the offshore reef.

THE BEST VIEW of the sea — home, Nugget Point, Southland.

COASTLINE NEAR Rapahoe, West Coast.

Norrie Groves, goldpanner

'There's snow on the hills, there's frost in the gully, that minds me of things that I've seen and done, of blokes that I knew, and mates that I've worked with, and the sprees we had in the days gone by.'   — David McKee Wright

Typical of the old-time panners is Norrie Groves (above), who lives near Dunedin but still seeks to strike it rich at Gillespies Beach.

Gillespies Beach is part of a rocky coast in the Westland National Park that experienced the gold rush days of the early 1800s. Sealers also went there, rampaging through the seal colony which only now is starting to recover.

Amid all this history, Norrie Groves offers a laconic and resolute image, still searching for gold long after the parade has passed.

NORRIE GROVES GETS down to work at Gillespies Beach.

NORRIE GROVES, goldpanner.

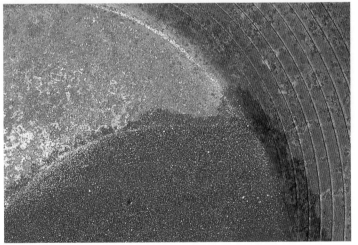

THE SEARCH FOR the sparkle in the pan.

Driftwood is strewn over the beach after a storm at Hicks Bay, East Cape.

HORSES LOOK SEAWARD on an East Cape promontory.

SHEEP AMID the morning fog, Kaikoura.

Come swift ship and welcome navigators. Link and line with your instruments this earth to heaven under the propitious stars.

M.K. Joseph, poet, novelist and scholar

LIGHTHOUSE ACROSS the sea, Castlepoint, Wairarapa.

A great land,
uplifted high

IN 1642, WHEN ABEL TASMAN sighted New Zealand he noted, 'Towards the middle of the day we saw a great land uplifted high. We had it S.E. of us, about sixty miles away.'

The Southern Alps are one of the glories of New Zealand. The alpine chain is a world crowned by constant cumulus cloud. It offers a thrilling vista of sentinels, dominated by the mighty Mt Cook and its neighbour Mt Tasman. From the high points, the world looks like an ice-capped sea.

Among the many breathtaking sights of the Alps are Franz Josef Glacier, at 11 kilometres long a shining river of ice rippling with white, green and blue. Some consider Fox Glacier, 13 kilometres long, an even grander spectacle, with its valley walls draped by a veil of waterfalls.

IMPOSING MT TASMAN, Westland National Park.

TOURISTS TREAD carefully on a guided walk on the Franz Josef Glacier.

GROUP PICTURE TIME at the base of Fox Glacier: 'Say freeze!'

A HELICOPTER deposits
tourists on the slopes of
Mt Cook National Park.

'IF YOU MUST bow your
head, let it be only to
the highest mountain.'
Mt Tasman and Mt Cook.

And now for something completely different

IN A THRILL-SEEKING WORLD, bungy-jumping is surely among the top ten pursuits to set the adrenalin really racing. Nor do you need much equipment — just yourself, a good set of nerves, and a special rope tied around your ankles. Once rigged up the rest is easy. All you do is fall, jump, dive or descend whatever way you choose.

Queenstown, sited in one of the most dramatic locations in the world, seems to be developing a reputation as the bungy-jumping capital of New Zealand. Luckily, for those after less heart-thudding thrills, there is a whole host of other entertainment on offer, from skiing and jet-boating to sedate trips on Lake Wakatipu on the TSS *Earnslaw*.

All at your fingertips — or ankles — you might say.

THE KAWARAU BRIDGE — a popular jumping-off place near Queenstown.

'YOU WANNA HAVE A GO?' Careful preparation and then it's a big jump backwards from Kawarau Bridge.

THERE'S LIFE after bungy jumping. Trampers explore the landscape near the Bridge to Nowhere, Whanganui National Park.

MORE THRILLS AHEAD. Whitewater rafting, Kaituna River, near Rotorua.

IF ALL ELSE FAILS, just look for fish. Algae, Knight's Point, West Coast.

FISHERMAN, Lake Moeraki, West Coast.

New Zealand's golden fleece

WHEREVER YOU GO in New Zealand you will always find sheep — over 50 million of them. They are 'the golden fleece', successfully introduced into New Zealand in 1834 and within a short time one of the cornerstones of the New Zealand economy.

With the introduction of refrigerated shipping in 1882, New Zealand shot ahead to become one of the world's leaders in the sheep industry. Today, sheep farming is a major income earner for everyone from the farmer to the shearer to the wool buyer to the retailer.

This is where it begins — on hot days at stations like Loch Linnhe, near Queenstown.

MUSTERERS BRING the sheep down from the high country and into the pens during sheep round-up, Loch Linnhe Station.

I come from a country electorate where life is not too complicated. Back there, when we see an animal that looks like a sheep, grows wool, and is not too bright, we decide it probably is a sheep.

— Ben Couch, former Minister of the Crown

IT'S DUSTY WORK. Typical scenes during sheep round-up, Loch Linnhe Station, one of many that link back to Central Otago's run-holding past and the saga of the great High Country sheep stations.

THE COLOURS indicate each sheep's destiny — purple means life, orange means a field trip to the freezing works.

WE MAKE great wines too. Chard Farm Winery nestles in the Kawarau Gorge near Queenstown, one of many wineries winning an international reputation for New Zealand wines.

THE SUN POURS a golden river of light across The Remarkables near Queenstown.

THE SUN RISES on Glendhu Bay, Lake Wanaka.

It was one of those days so clear, so silent, so still, you almost feel the earth itself has stopped in astonishment at its own beauty.

— Katherine Mansfield, short story writer

An ember shaken from Maui's foot

THE MAORI SAY that after Maui had fished up the land he took a step onto the North Island. His feet caught up some of the fire that was burning on it. His first reaction was to shake his feet, and the fire fell into the sea, creating the island known as Whakaari to the Maori but renamed White Island by Captain Cook.

The island is a reminder that New Zealand is on the 'Rim of Fire' around the Pacific Basin. It is a volcano which still occasionally sends up steam and lava just to remind us it is active. This didn't stop sulphur being mined intermittently between 1885 and 1936, and old mining equipment is still evident on the island.

The island's isolation has provided Australian gannets with a place to nest on the slopes to the south.

THE GANNET COLONY on White Island. Below, detail of the volcanic landscape and, to the right, abandoned mining equipment.

THE RUGGED landscape of
White Island.

VOLCANIC MAJESTY —
White Island.

THE COLOSSAL crack across the land, all that is left from the day when Mount Tarawera exploded, 10 June 1886.

THE DECEPTIVELY TRANQUIL crater lake which crowns Mount Ruapehu, Tongariro National Park.

AND EVERYWHERE there are waterfalls — Sterling Falls, Milford Sound.

TARANAKI FALLS, Tongariro National Park.

LAKE MATHESON, Westland National Park. Sometimes, if the surface is perfect, you cannot tell the real from the reflection.

Have you done the track?

MOST NEW ZEALANDERS have done it or plan to do it, and every visitor to New Zealand should do it — walk the 54-kilometre Milford Track. Even when it rains, and the rivers rise, it's not enough to dampen the spirits.

The track follows the overland route into Milford pioneered by explorer Quintin MacKinnon in 1888. The Government, in 1913, decided to turn the route into a tourist track at the suggestion of explorer Thomas Mackenzie who said, 'The overland route to the Sutherland Falls and the Milford Sound will be practicable in summer after cutting a track. The scenery is simply magnificent.'

Since those days thousands of walkers have been attracted to walk the Milford Track. The bush is embellished with moss and spiked with tree ferns of remarkable luminosity. The alpine country allows vistas over craggy peaks for as far as the eye can see. The immensity of the universe is all there for the taking, and at the end of it all is a great sense of personal achievement and camaraderie.

Ready to go?

HEADING OUT to the start of the Milford Track on the *Tawera*. Did we forget to tell you that sometimes it rains?

TRAMPERS, MACKINNON
Pass, the Milford Track. The
pass is named after pioneer
Quintin MacKinnon, who
blazed the overland route
into Milford.

Moss, TREEFERNS and trampers — the magic unfolds as trampers traverse the Milford Track.

SWEATY WORK but, ah, the sights are worth it! Scenes along the way, and walking boots at Sandfly Point, the end of the Track.

AND THERE, AHEAD, are the Fiords. Journey's end, Mitre Peak, Milford Sound.

MA TE ATUA koe e manaaki
— go well in the world.

My mother was the earth, my father was the sky. They were Rangi and Papa, the first parents, whose children were born into darkness until the time of Separation and the dawning of the first day.

— Witi Ihimaera, novelist

Photographic notes

The photographs in this book were taken with the following equipment:

Leica M6 with 1:2.0/35 and 1:1.4/75 Summicron-M lenses.
Nikon F90 and F801s with 1:2.8/20, 1:3.3/24-50, 1:2.8/105
Macro, and 1:2.8/80-200 AF Nikkor lenses, along with a
Nikon Speedlight SB-24 flash.
Widelux F8 panorama camera
Bogen 3221 tripod — heavy, bulky, yet invaluable.

The images were photographed on Fujichrome RDP-100
Professional Film.

Acknowledgements

Thank you to the many New Zealanders who welcomed
me to Aotearoa and made me feel at home. And thank you,
friends and fellow travellers, for the inspiration and the best
of times. You know who you are.

— H.L.

Thanks to Montana Wines Ltd and Air New Zealand for
travel assistance in the South Island, and to Holger Leue,
Ian Watt, Susan Brierley, Chris Lipscombe and Alison Jacobs.

— W.I.

Also by Holger Leue:

Epiphyllum — The Splendor of Leaf Cacti (1987)
The Legendary Land (1994)
Land Sea & Sky (1994)

Also by Witi Ihimaera:

Pounamu, Pounamu (1972)
Tangi (1973)
Whanau (1974)
The New Net Goes Fishing (1977)
Into the World of Light (ed. with D.S. Long, 1982)
The Matriarch (1986)
The Whale Rider (1987)
Dear Miss Mansfield (1989)
Te Ao Marama (ed., 5 volumes, 1992–)
Bulibasha, King of the Gypsies (1994)
The Legendary Land (1994)
Land Sea & Sky (1994)
Nights in the Gardens of Spain (1995)